Brown
at the
Zoo

by Christianne C. Jones

illustrated by Todd Ouren

Special thanks to our advisers for their expertise:

Linda Frichtel, Design Adjunct Faculty
Minneapolis College of Art & Design

Terry Flaherty, Ph.D., Professor of English
Minnesota State University, Mankato

 PICTURE WINDOW BOOKS
Minneapolis, Minnesota

Editor: Jill Kalz
Designer: Hilary Wacholz
Page Production: Melissa Kes
Art Director: Nathan Gassman
The illustrations in this book were created digitally.

Picture Window Books
5115 Excelsior Boulevard
Suite 232
Minneapolis, MN 55416
877-845-8392
www.picturewindowbooks.com

Printed in the United States of America.

All books published by Picture Window Books
are manufactured with paper containing at least
10 percent post-consumer waste.

Library of Congress Cataloging-in-Publication Data
Jones, Christianne C.
Brown at the zoo / by Christianne C. Jones ; illustrated by
Todd Ouren.
p. cm. — (Know your colors)
ISBN-13: 978-1-4048-3765-2 (library binding)
ISBN-10: 1-4048-3765-5 (library binding)
1. Brown—Juvenile literature. 2. Colors—Juvenile literature.
I. Ouren, Todd, ill. II. Title.
QC495.5.J6566 2008
535.6—dc22   2007004277

The world is filled with COLORS.

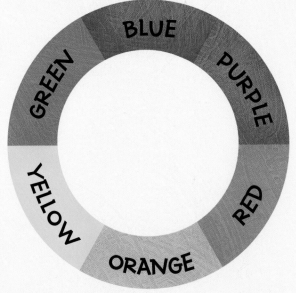

Colors are either primary or secondary. Red, yellow, and blue are primary colors. These are the colors that can't be made by mixing two other colors together. Orange, purple, and green are secondary colors. Secondary colors are made by mixing together two primary colors.

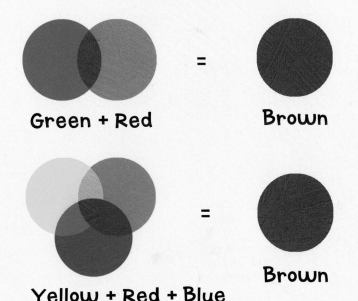

Green + Red = Brown

Yellow + Red + Blue = Brown

Brown is neither primary nor secondary. It is a tertiary color. Mixing a primary color (for example, red) with the secondary color that lies opposite it on the color wheel (in this case, green) makes brown. Mixing all three primary colors together also makes brown.

Keep your eyes open for colorful fun!

4

The color **BROWN** lives in the zoo with lions, bears, and a monkey or two.

Fuzzy **BROWN** bears snooze in a cave.

6

8

Funny **BROWN** monkeys refuse to behave.

A golden **BROWN** lion lets out a roar.

Busy **BROWN** squirrels love to explore.

Bouncy **BROWN** kangaroos jump, jump, jump.

A lazy **BROWN** camel has one big hump.

A graceful **BROWN** eagle flies to its nest.

A long **BROWN** broom sweeps up the mess.

It's the end of the day for the animals and crew.
Where else can **BROWN** be found at the zoo?

MAKING BROWN

WHAT YOU NEED:
- red paint
- paper plates
- green paint
- paintbrushes
- yellow paint
- blue paint

WHAT YOU DO:
1. Place a few drops of red paint on a paper plate.
2. Add a few drops of green paint to the red paint.
3. Mix the red and green paint together with a brush to make brown.
4. Now, repeat the steps using the red, yellow, and blue paint. How is this brown different than the first brown you made?

TO LEARN MORE

AT THE LIBRARY
Dahl, Michael. *Brown: Seeing Brown All Around Us.* Mankato, Minn.: Capstone Press, 2005.

Mitchell, Melanie. *Brown.* Minneapolis: Lerner, 2004.

Whitehouse, Patricia. *Brown Foods.* Chicago: Heinemann, 2004.

ON THE WEB
FactHound offers a safe, fun way to find Web sites related to this book. All of the sites on FactHound have been researched by our staff.

1. Visit *www.facthound.com*
2. Type in this special code: 1404837655
3. Click on the FETCH IT button.

Your trusty FactHound will fetch the best sites for you!

FUN FACTS

- Brown is often called a nature color. It is the color of dirt, wood, and leather.

- A lot of restaurants use the color brown in their decorations because it can stimulate, or start up, your appetite.

- A baked pudding made from apples, bread crumbs, and spices is called a brown Betty.

- More than 98 percent of all brown bears in the United States live in Alaska.

Look for all of the books in the Know Your Colors series:

Autumn Orange
Batty for Black
Big Red Farm
Brown at the Zoo
Camping in Green
Hello, Yellow!
Pink Takes a Bow
Purple Pride
Splish, Splash, and Blue
Winter White